WINNING AT WORK READINESS

STEP-BY-STEP GUIDE TO

PROBLEM SOLVING AT SCHOOL & WORK

Larry Gerber

WITHDRAWN

ROSEN
PUBLISHING®

New York

D0049956

Published in 2015 by The Rosen Publishing Group, Inc.
29 East 21st Street, New York, NY 10010

Copyright © 2015 by The Rosen Publishing Group, Inc.

First Edition

Library of Congress Cataloging-in-Publication Data

Gerber, Larry, 1946–
Step-by-step guide to problem solving at school & work/Larry Gerber. — First edition.
    pages cm. — (Winning at work readiness)
Includes bibliographical references and index.
ISBN 978-1-4777-7782-4 (library bound) — ISBN 978-1-4777-7783-1 (pbk.)
— ISBN 978-1-4777-7784-8 (6-pack)
1. Problem solving—Juvenile literature. 2. Problem solving in children—Juvenile literature. I. Title. II. Title: Step-by-step guide to problem solving at school and work.
BF723.P8G47 2015
153.4'3—dc23

                                                                    2014006341

Manufactured in the United States of America

CONTENTS

INTRODUCTION

Problem solving is a skill that everybody needs, whether it's at school or at work, in relationships or friendships, or just in everyday life. It has even been said that problem solving is a necessary skill for students and employees to succeed in the world. Actually, problem solving is a skill that we all need just to get by.

Everybody is a problem solver at some point or another. It's not necessary to have a college degree or straight As on your report card. Thousands of years before the invention of writing, prehistoric peoples were solving fundamental problems, such as acquiring food, water, and shelter, just to name a few.

Problem solving is a part of daily life, and while some people may be better at it than others, we all do it, often without even really thinking about it. Even better news is that anybody can learn to be a better problem solver. Like most skills, it gets easier with practice.

Anyone who has ever tried to reach the next level in a video game or studied for a math exam is actually developing problem-solving skills. Those skills can really pay off, whether it's a matter of succeeding in school or finding a good job and succeeding at it.

Employees who can handle problems prosper on the job. They also tend to impress their superiors, given that they can readily fix problems that arise on the job without being overly dependent on others for help. On job applications and proficiency tests, as well as in interviews, employers oftentimes look for evidence that the applicant excels at problem solving.

Sometimes the thought process behind solving a problem seems automatic. Imagine a young boy riding a bike who suddenly notices a big hole in the path ahead and swerves to avoid it. It may

Although you may not realize it, you are solving problems as you play video games and try to improve your score.

seem intuitive, but observing the hole and swerving around it was a problem-solving process. Finding solutions to problems like that is practically automatic. That is because quick problem solving makes use of both practice and experience. The bike rider probably took a few falls when learning how to ride a bike. He almost certainly got advice from somebody—either parents or friends—when starting out. These experiences contributed to his decision to swerve around the hole and avoid falling.

Many small everyday problems can be solved quickly. Some problems take longer to work out, but that's not necessarily a bad thing. Depending on the complexity of the problem, careless, easy fixes can sometimes cause more problems than they solve. While it would be convenient to have a one-size-fits-all formula for solving problems, there truly is no such thing. Problems come in all shapes and sizes, and so do solutions.

The great news is that many people have worked out all sorts of ways to handle the types of problems that commonly come up in practically all fields of work and study. Their experiences can come in handy for everyone. Some methods are more complicated than others, but most of them have several steps in common. In the pages that follow we will review some of the essential steps to becoming an excellent problem solver at school and on the job.

Chapter 1

"HOUSTON, WE'VE HAD A PROBLEM"

In April 1970, the American spacecraft *Apollo 13* was 200,000 miles (322,000 kilometers) from Earth and nearing the moon when warning lights came on in the cabin and the ship began to shudder. Astronaut Jack Swigert sent a clear radio message to NASA Mission Control located in Houston, Texas: "Houston, we've had a problem."

Things got scary fast. It soon became obvious that the spacecraft and the three astronauts aboard were in serious trouble. The mysterious accident had crippled the ship, causing it to run low on fuel, power, oxygen, and water. These low levels meant that the spacecraft couldn't maneuver properly. The planned landing on the moon was scrubbed. It wasn't even certain that the astronauts could make it back to Earth.

In the hours that followed, hundreds of experts went into action, working desperately to find a way to bring the crew home safely. The initial problem was later traced to faulty wiring, which caused a spark and a fire in an oxygen tank, but the source of the problem wasn't immediately clear at the time. What was certain was that the fault had triggered a long and complicated list of other problems, all of which needed to be identified and solved in order to prevent a fatal disaster.

Experts in electronics, math, computers, engineering, and aeronautics scrambled into action. They identified the biggest question—how to get the astronauts back to Earth safely—and broke it down into smaller, more manageable problems. Each team

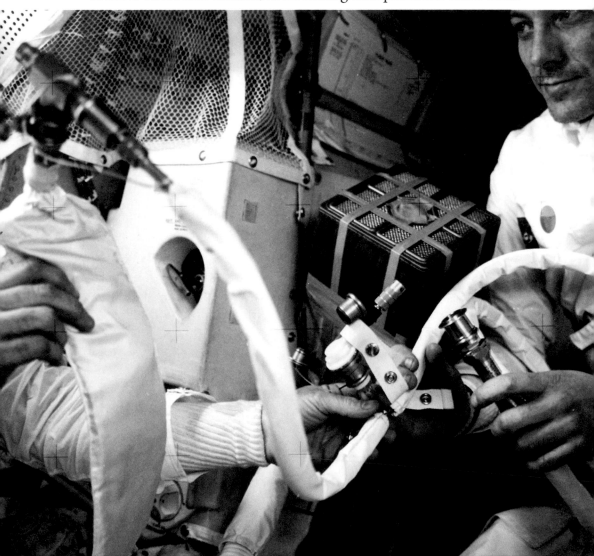

Jack Swigert (*right*) and his fellow astronauts had to build a new apparatus to scrub carbon dioxide from the spacecraft after an oxygen tank exploded.

of experts tackled the problem that they understood best. They came up with possible solutions to each problem, evaluated them, selected one, and then implemented it.

In the end, the astronauts and the ground teams in Houston came up with a set of shortcuts and provisional solutions sufficient for bringing the damaged spacecraft back to Earth. The *Apollo 13* story is one of history's most famous and most dramatic examples of problem solving.

THE "WHERE" AND "WHAT" OF PROBLEMS

The problems that most people face are a lot more down-to-earth than the *Apollo 13* crisis, and they're usually not as dramatic. Nonetheless, when we are faced with tough situations—whether they occur at home, school, or work—finding answers can seem every bit as important and complicated as they did on that 1970 space mission. When you're in the middle of a problem, and it is your problem, it can seem like a very big deal indeed.

Problems tend to have a bad reputation, but the truth is that it is hard to imagine where we would be without them. In reality, life itself can be thought of as a series of problems, most of which are pretty easily solved. It starts at birth. When newborn babies get hungry, they cry. Once they are fed, that problem is solved. This simple process illustrates a problem-solving technique. When babies are confronted with the problem—their hunger—they cry. Crying attracts the attention of adults, who can then feed them, thus solving their problem. Crying, therefore, is an important problem-solving technique for hungry babies.

While problems can seem overwhelming in the moment, life would actually be pretty dull without problems. That is why sometimes people invent them. Sports and games are effectively

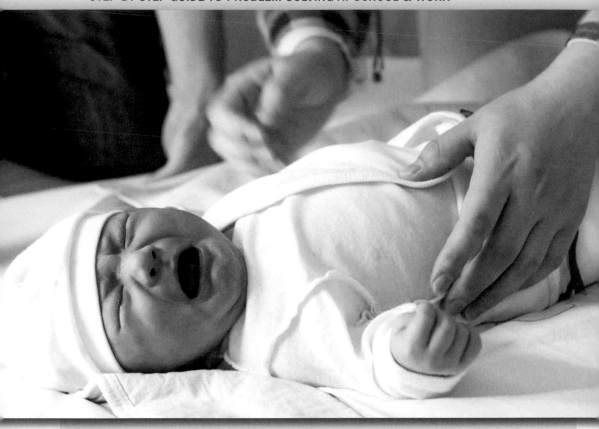

Even infants have problems and strategies for solving them, as this baby's crying has alerted an adult who can provide comfort.

just exercises in problem solving. It may be a matter of defeating an opponent on the playing field, or it may mean driving, flying, or shooting straight in a video game. Either way, these recreational activities are scenarios in which people actively create a problem to be solved for fun.

With movies, books, and TV shows, people sit back and watch story characters work their way through their own problems. By observing a character dealing with a problem and guessing how he or she will solve it, problem solving becomes a fun activity, just as in sports or video games. Most importantly, even when problems are not fun, many of the problems people face have a positive side to them: solving them generally makes a person stronger, smarter,

and happier. That's true even when a problem is downright dangerous, such as on *Apollo 13*.

One could ask how the *Apollo 13* crisis made anybody stronger
or smarter. The answer is simple: after NASA determined exactly
what went wrong, engineers improved the spacecraft's design to
avoid that flaw. Future missions had better wiring and a backup
oxygen tank. As a result, that problem didn't happen again.

WHO CARES?

Another important example of problems that people seek out to
improve their skills are those faced by students at school, such as
math problems or exam questions. These exercises are designed to
help make students smarter. Sometimes they can be tricky or hard,
but there is no great secret to dealing with them. By simply showing up for class, paying attention to the teacher, doing homework,
studying, and asking questions, a student has a clear formula for
dealing with practice problems.

Situations get a little more challenging when problems involve
other people, especially when other people themselves are the
problems. Bullies are a good example of people who can be a
problem at school. People whom you might need to depend on
but cannot, such as a friend with a drug or alcohol problem, or a
friend who is dishonest, are other examples of people who can be
a problem.

Dealing with problems with other people can be difficult even
when the issues are relatively simple. When a student is a member
of a club or on the student council, for instance, or even just trying
to decide on something with a group of friends, it is important to
hear what each person has to say, even if others' ideas don't seem
very practical. When people feel as though they are a part of the
team, they are more likely to accept the final decision the group
reaches and do their best to make it work.

Problem solving is also essential for getting good jobs and performing well at them. Just finding a job can be a puzzler for many people. However, basic problem-solving steps can help someone find a paying job and also handle the stressful situations that may come up at work.

Oftentimes, the "problem situations" a worker encounters on the job are just a normal part of the daily work routine—the normal tasks that employees are expected to complete in exchange for their pay. However, smart workers can get ahead by applying problem-solving skills to situations that are not necessarily spelled out in their everyday duties. It may entail identifying a problem that others miss or coming up with creative ways to handle more obvious, although difficult, problems.

THE BASIC STEPS

Some methods for problem solving include multiple steps and diagrams. Many fields of study, such as math and computer science, have their own special languages and alphabets for solving problems. Many of the books and online articles on problem solving deal with situations that come up in companies and other organizations. They often focus on situations involving groups of people. Problem solving doesn't have to be a complicated process, however. Whether the issue involves other people or is something to be handled by one person on his or her own, there are five basic steps that work in most problematic situations.

The first step is to identify the problem. This step seems so obvious that it is often tempting to skip over it. A lot of the time people want a solution so badly that they don't actually take the time to form a clear idea of just what it is that needs to be solved. Collecting information about the problem and defining it in simple terms can save a lot of work and prevent mistakes. It will also help in communicating the problem to other people.

THE DIRTY DISH THAT SAVED LIVES

The Scottish scientist Sir Alexander Fleming was rather messy. In 1928, he took a vacation from his research work at a London hospital, where he was trying to find a medicine that could stop killer bacteria. He came back after two weeks to find a problem in his lab. The petri dishes that he had been using to grow bacteria were lying around in a jumble where he had left them, dirty and contaminated. Fleming would have to clean them and start from scratch.

Fleming was putting the dishes into a cleaning solution when he noticed something strange on one of the dishes. Mold was growing on it—which wasn't too unusual—except that the mold had killed some of the staph bacteria in the dish. Instead of cleaning that dish with the others, Fleming took a sample of the mold. He studied it and found that it came from the *Penicillium* genus. He wrote a paper on what he named "penicillin" and how it killed bacteria.

Before Fleming's accidental discovery, there was no cure for life-threatening illnesses such as pneumonia and rheumatic fever. Even a cut or a scratch could be fatal if it became infected. Penicillin was dubbed the "wonder drug," and it led to a new age of medical antibiotics. Scientists in the United Kingdom and the United States developed enough penicillin to save thousands of lives during World War II. Penicillin and similar antibiotics are still saving lives today.

Next, it is helpful to make a list of possible solutions. While it could seem convenient if every problem's solution were obvious, the truth is that we wouldn't grow much or learn from our problem-solving experiences. If the problem involves other

By listening to each other's ideas, you and your friends will be able to find a solution that suits all of you.

people, it is a good idea to ask them for suggestions when coming up with possible solutions. This is the "brainstorming" step, the

stage for coming up with as many ideas as possible regardless of whether or not it seems likely that they will work out. This second step is the time to get creative.

The third step is to evaluate the alternatives. This is the time to examine and ask questions about each of the possible solutions. Is a solution possible? Is it practical? Will it truly solve the problem? How will a certain solution affect other people? How will it affect me? Is there an easier or cheaper way? Is there a more thorough way? All of these could be included on the list of basic questions that a person should ask himself or herself during step three.

The fourth step is for the problem solver to make a decision. This may seem like the toughest part of the process, but having completed the previous three steps thoroughly often makes it easier to choose the best plan of action. By the time somebody needs to make a decision, he or she will have already created a list of possibilities and weighed the benefits and disadvantages of each decision. These objective measures can help easily resolve which is the best solution.

Finally, the time comes to put a decision into practice. This stage entails making a plan and carrying it out. It also implies changes and paying attention to how well the changes are working to solve the problem. By mastering this process and learning how to come up with and implement creative solutions, anybody can become an expert problem solver and shine in school or at work.

Chapter 2

WHAT'S GOING ON HERE?

When something goes wrong, it can be very tempting to try to fix it right away. If there is a problem to solve or a decision to make, sometimes the first instinct is to react urgently, and a voice inside yells, "Do something now!" But acting right away may not be the best idea, especially if it is not clear yet what caused the problem or even what exactly is wrong. Getting a clear definition of a problem is often the first step toward solving it, and it's an important step.

The most brilliant solutions won't help much if they are applied to the wrong problems. Albert Einstein is popularly quoted as having once said that if he had just one hour to save the world, he would spend fifty-five minutes defining the problem and only five minutes solving it.

DEFINING THE PROBLEM

Problems are so commonplace in everyday life that sometimes they are practically invisible. At one time or another, nearly everyone has heard somebody say the phrase, "I know something's wrong, but I can't put my finger on it." Often what that means is that the

Without problem-solving skills, Albert Einstein never would have developed his theory of relativity, which revolutionized the study of physics.

speaker is so involved in whatever is happening that he or she can't recognize the problem. Sometimes the problems that are closest to us are the hardest ones to identify. Nonetheless, just recognizing them is an important skill in and of itself.

In the business world, there is a whole profession designed around recognizing and solving problems. Consultants can make millions of dollars each year by visiting companies where things don't seem to be going well, taking a look at what is happening,

17

WHAT'S YOUR TYPE?

Psychologists have known for a long time that people tend to follow certain patterns in how they prefer to take in information, solve problems, and make decisions. Following in the footsteps of the work of Swiss psychiatrist Carl Jung, Isabel Briggs Myers and her mother, Katharine Cook Briggs, came up with sixteen different personality types based on those patterns. Four of these types are "sensing," "intuition," "thinking," and "feeling." For example, some people prefer to focus strictly on the basic information perceived by their senses, mainly sight and hearing, while others rely more on intuition to add meaning to the information they receive. When making decisions, some people prefer thinking logically while others are more likely to consider feelings—both their own and those of other people.

To solve problems and make decisions, psychologists recommend using each of those processes in turn. The first step is sensing, which includes looking at the facts without drawing any conclusions or judgment. Then, using intuition, look at all the possibilities, brainstorm ideas, and see if any solutions seem to present themselves as more obvious than others. Next, think logically about what was discovered through both sensing and intuition. Applying logic at this stage entails separating the sure facts from things that are uncertain, as well as considering the pros and cons of each possibility. Finally, consider how you feel about the choices. Think about how the decision will affect others and how they will feel about it.

talking to people, and creating a report on what some of the principal problems are. Consultants will also make recommendations on how to improve the situation, but the biggest part of their job is simply defining the problem.

Business consultants are outsiders, meaning they do not work in the companies that hire them. They can often see what insiders—the routine employees who work at the company—cannot see because they are looking at the problems with fresh eyes. Obviously, most people cannot afford to hire consultants to define their day-to-day personal problems, but they can try to look at the issues with fresh eyes by using a few mental tricks.

One great trick is to pretend that the problem belongs to somebody else. This method allows people to see the issue from another angle. Putting some distance between oneself and the issue at hand is another useful trick. Everything seems smaller, and less intimidating, when it is seen from farther away. Another trick is to evaluate whether or not the problem is truly a big deal. Some problems may be only a minor inconvenience and may not really need so much focus and energy. As the adage goes, "Don't sweat the small stuff!"

PROBLEM OR SYMPTOM?

When newfound problems are hard to define, an important question ought to arise: is this issue the real problem, or is it just a symptom of another bigger problem? For instance, when the *Apollo 13* spacecraft began to shudder, the crew knew right away that something was wrong. The shaking, loss of power, lack of oxygen and water, and several mechanical failures each seemed like an overwhelming problem on their own, but in reality they were all just symptoms of a sole, basic problem. It was only later, after the crew had returned to Earth, that investigators found the root cause of all the trouble: faulty wiring in an oxygen tank.

It is often hard to see the root problem, especially when things are changing quickly or when things that used to work suddenly stop working. To discover the root cause of a problem, it can be helpful to think the way that a doctor does. Physicians diagnose illness by gathering information. They examine patients, consider the symptoms, and figure out what could be causing them. The patient may have symptoms such as a fever or a cough, but the doctor wouldn't know what to prescribe without knowing what illness is the cause of the symptoms first. Doctors also ask several "where," "what," "when," and "how" questions during a patient's visit. When did the symptoms begin? What have you been eating and drinking recently? Have you been anywhere where another person was ill? How much sleep have you had recently?

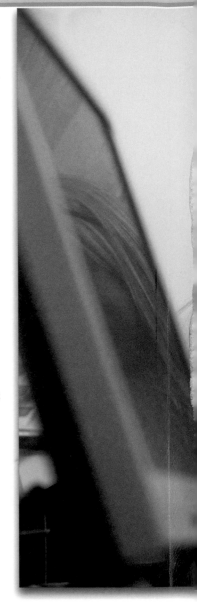

Asking questions helps peel away the outer problems—the symptoms—to find the one base issue that really needs a solution. Some experts reduce the series of questions further. They suggest simply asking, "Why?" Doing so often leads to more questions, but the trick is to keep asking why until the root cause is reached.

Here's an example of how this method works. Let's imagine a teen whose parents won't let him go out with his friends on the weekend. The problem seems to be that he cannot go out on the weekend. Nonetheless, asking why he cannot go out will lead to the conclusion that his parents are upset with him. Subsequently

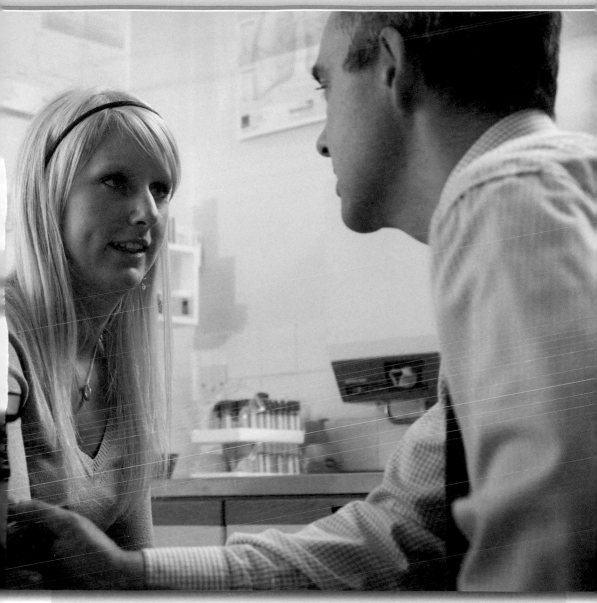

At a doctor's appointment, your description of your symptoms helps the physician arrive at a diagnosis and treatment plan for you.

asking why his parents are upset could lead to the explanation that the boy didn't do well on a recent exam. So then he needs to ask himself why he did poorly on the exam. The answer might be that he didn't have time to study, and the answer to that "why" might be because he has a part-time job and couldn't prepare for his exam.

After a series of basic questions, it was easy to identify that an overcrowded schedule was the root problem. There might be any number of ways to solve the problem, including working fewer hours, managing his free time on the weekends better, or changing other aspects of his schedule. But none of these problems would have presented themselves if the problem had not first been defined.

QUESTIONS ASKED, PROBLEMS SOLVED

When faced with an important problem to solve, asking basic, common questions like those mentioned above is always helpful, and if others are involved, it is also key to ask them questions as well. Asking for help from a trusted source, even if he or she is not directly involved with the problem, may also be helpful. Different people may have different ideas about the situation.

The following are some examples of questions that can help define problems. Some are obvious, some not so obvious:

> ❯ What is the main problem?
> ❯ Is it my responsibility to solve this problem?
> ❯ How long has it been a problem?
> ❯ Why did the problem start?
> ❯ Have others had this same problem?
> ❯ Will it fix itself if I ignore it?

The point of questions such as these is to get such a clear idea of the problem that it is possible to describe it in a simple sentence.

A good start is saying or writing, "The problem is...", and then filling in the blank.

PUTTING PROBLEM-SOLVING SKILLS TO WORK

Being able to define problems is more than just the first step in solving them. It is also a valuable skill when it comes to applying for a job. Even if it is not an explicit part of the job description,

At a job interview, you should be prepared to give examples of specific issues you've resolved in the past, which will show the hiring manager that you can tackle problems effectively.

employers in just about every field like to see candidates who can prove they've identified problems and solved them in creative ways.

Just claiming to be great at identifying and solving problems probably will not help much. It is much better to have one or even multiple specific examples. Being able to describe a problem that came up or a difficult task tackled in a reasonably detailed manner is bound to impress a prospective employer. It is also impressive to highlight the positive results that came about because of the problem solving.

Organizing a car wash is a great way to raise money for a good cause and also showcase your problem-solving skills.

It doesn't require a lot of work experience for an applicant to show that he or she is capable of defining and solving problems. Furthermore, the problems that an applicant has handled do not necessarily have to relate to the job for which he or she is applying. It is the ability to understand and deal with problems that matters.

Organizing a school trip, raising money for a cause or group, straightening out a computer problem, finding advertisers for a website, dealing with a difficult customer at a previous job, or working on a student council committee to resolve an issue are a few of the many ways in which new graduates and others may have developed problem-solving skills that look good on a job résumé or application.

People who have worked as part of a problem-solving team should explain their contribution toward finding a solution. Team players are attractive job candidates. Offering evidence that a person helped find a new or different way to overcome a problem is prized by employers because it demonstrates both creativity and innovation, two essential job qualities in any field.

Chapter 3

LIST IT AND LIKE IT...OR NOT

W hile logic is often the biggest help in defining problems, imagination is arguably the most important factor when solving them. The ability to "think outside the box," which means not in the usual or expected way, is an asset in just about every profession or subject area at school. This skill is especially valuable in the second step of the problem-solving process.

Once there is a clear definition of the problem, it is time to move on to the next step—thinking up as many ways as possible to solve the problem and making a list of them. Before even starting on the list, however, there is something important—and counterintuitive—to do, which is to forget about the problem entirely for awhile. That may sound all wrong, but it is actually very hard to think about solutions when the mind is focused on a problem. And step two is all about solutions, both coming up with a variety of possible ones and also judging each one individually.

BRAINSTORMING

One of the most common tools for coming up with alternative solutions is brainstorming. In companies and in organizations,

In a brainstorming meeting, everyone's input is valuable because more ideas lead to a greater chance that one of them will be successful.

brainstorming is usually done in meetings. Everybody involved with the problem gets together, often around a table, and writes down or mentions as many possible solutions as they can think of. Brainstorming works well in a group because more people can come up with more alternatives. You can also brainstorm by yourself, however. The more ideas you can come up with, the better. Some of them obviously won't work, but that's not the important thing at this stage. Listing as many alternatives as possible helps open the mind to new ideas, and sometimes aspects of an idea that will not work lead to another solution that, in fact, could work.

Even if some of the solutions sound ridiculous, this is not the step to judge them. At this point, every idea should be listed. It's important to keep an open mind and think creatively. A common mistake is trying to evaluate alternatives as they come up. For now, a successful problem solver is simply trying to list as many alternatives as possible.

In group brainstorming sessions, a generally positive rule is that members should never make fun of the ideas that others present. Thinking about what may seem like an outrageous alternative might lead to another idea that isn't so outrageous after all—one that might actually work! Some alternatives might also be unappealing. They could be things that other members of the group wouldn't want to do or wouldn't like. These unappealing alternatives need to be listed anyway. In this step, there are no bad ideas. Every idea is valid.

Let's look at the example of the teen with an overcrowded schedule. There are lots of possible solutions to this problem. They include quitting an extracurricular activity like basketball or asking to work fewer hours at his part-time job, just for starters. Perhaps he might try talking to teachers to see if his courses could be scheduled differently so multiple exams don't happen around the same time. Finding a new job that requires fewer work hours might be on the list, too, or finding a job that is closer to school or home, so it won't take so long to travel to and from work.

The key question to keep asking is, "What if?" It also couldn't hurt to ask other people for their opinions and ideas. If those people are involved in the problem, it is not only helpful, but also essential to talk to them. In the example of the busy schedule, the boy's teachers, boss, basketball coach, and parents all have a stake in solving the problem. Finding out if they have any possible solutions could lead to ideas the student himself would not have otherwise come up with.

Another helpful tip is to find someone else who has had the same or a similar problem. Somebody who has been through the same situation can share what he or she did to solve the problem. This solution might be something the questioner had never thought of before.

If the problem isn't urgent, it might also help to set the list of solutions aside for a few days. Forgetting about the old ideas and coming up with some entirely new ones from a fresh perspective is an excellent approach, if there is time. Adding these new solutions to the list of other ideas will create an expanding pool of options. The more ideas one has, the better the solution is likely to be.

MAKING THE GOAL

Some of the possible solutions on the list will surely look better than others, and it's probably obvious that some won't work at all. Before trying to decide on the best ones, however, it helps to write down a couple of other factors: goals and priorities.

A goal is simply a statement of what a person is trying to achieve. With the example of the overcrowded schedule, the goal would be to balance all activities so that there is time for study, time for work, and time for recreation.

Setting priorities means arranging things in order of importance. If the root problem is a lack of study time, then that would have the highest priority. Other activities would then be listed in order of their importance after study time.

Consider all the alternatives on the list, one by one. People need to consider if each solution will actually solve the problem or if it needs to be combined with other actions to solve the issues. Other considerations are whether the solution is reasonable and possible, and whether or not the solution might actually cause new, additional problems in the future. Getting more information

Writing down a list of goals is a good way to determine what is most important to you and how you can achieve those things.

about some of the alternatives might be necessary before a decision can be made.

Finding the right solution often means compromising. Even the best solution may not be ideal, and few solutions are ever perfect. Combining alternatives is one way to compromise. In the busy schedule example, that might mean cutting back on work hours and also asking to leave sports practice early once a week. Another compromise might be to sacrifice some weekend free time to study.

THE SMELL TEST

Problem-solving steps are designed mostly to help people arrive at the best solution. The common questions that need to be answered when considering possible solutions are, "Will it solve the problem?," "Is it a reasonable or possible solution?," and "Will it get me what I want?" Sometimes there are other questions that need answering, however. These include, "Is it right?" as well as, "Is it fair?" Those are ethical questions.

Business leaders and other decision makers often do an exercise called the "smell test" to see whether or not they are solving a problem in a way that is fair to everyone concerned but that also doesn't compromise their own moral standards of good and bad. The smell test is a quick way to get a sense of whether or not something is the right thing.

Sorting out the difference between what is right, what works, and what you want isn't always easy. Experts and philosophers through the ages have written a lot about making ethical choices. Their work has suggested several other questions to help make tough choices. Here are just a few of them:

> Which option will do the most good and the least harm?

> Which option best respects the rights of everyone involved?

> Which option treats people equally and fairly?

> Which option is best for everyone, not just a few people?

> Which option helps me be the sort of person I want to be?

GETTING BUY-IN FROM OTHERS

Choosing an alternative, or a combination of options, can be pretty simple if there is only one person who is affected. Situations don't usually work that way, however. One person's decisions tend to ripple out and affect other people. Before trying to put a decision into practice, it may be necessary to see if others will accept it.

The ideal, or best, type of solution to a problem that involves more than one person is called a "win-win" solution. This involves agreements that make it possible for everyone to get at least something that they wanted. Win-win solutions are possible only when everyone involved is willing to listen to the needs of others and talk about ways to meet them. Negotiations that try to achieve a win-win solution aren't about defending a position or proving who is right and who is wrong. They focus more on figuring out how everyone can gain something from the discussion.

In the early twentieth century, management expert Mary Parker Follett told a story about two sisters quarreling over an orange. They kept arguing until their mother simply sliced the orange in half and gave them each an equal piece. One sister wanted orange juice, so she squeezed out her half and threw away the peel. The other wanted the peel to use in a recipe, so she grated up her half of the peel to cook with and threw away the flesh of the orange. If the sisters had been willing to listen to each other's needs instead of just arguing, they could have reached a win-win solution. One could have squeezed more juice from the whole orange, and the other could have had the whole peel for her recipe.

Sometimes people have to "sell" their idea, or emphasize all of its good points, to others who are involved. Believe it or not, experts say one of the best ways to sell an idea is *not* by trying to

Negotiation is key to any successful business decision. Everyone around the table needs to work together to agree upon the best solution.

talk someone into something! Instead, being a good listener is the best approach. For instance, asking someone, "How can I fix this?" or "What would happen if I tried this?" coupled with actively listening to his or her concerns and ideas will make the other person feel included in the process. If the person is contributing to a solution this way, then he or she is more likely to buy into it and help make it work.

Chapter 4

DECISIONS, DECISIONS

Making decisions is such an important part of problem solving that many people think that is what it is all about. Business executives, managers, coaches, and others earn their pay and their reputations based on how well they make decisions. However, anyone who has taken the earlier steps in the problem-solving process—defining the problem, listing every possible solution, and evaluating those possibilities—will likely find that making an actual decision comes a lot easier. Furthermore, that decision will be a lot more likely to work.

THE ANCIENT ART OF LOGIC

Logic is the most common decision-making tool, as well as one of the oldest. Logic is the use of reasoning to reach valid conclusions, often using statements and arguments. The word "argument," when used in logic, doesn't mean a disagreement. It is simply a way of putting ideas together, in step-by-step order, to reach a conclusion that makes sense.

Logic is used in every science and practically every field of study and profession. Employers value applicants who can show

Aristotle, a Greek philosopher in the fourth century BCE, is widely considered the founder of logic.

that they are logical thinkers because that means that they are likely to be good problem solvers. Logic helps people see patterns of good reasoning and faulty reasoning so they know which trains of thought to follow and which to avoid. It is not only a problem-solving tool, but it helps develop critical thinking, which is a big asset in all kinds of work, in study, and in everyday life.

STARTING, AND FINISHING, AN ARGUMENT

Logic focuses on the validity of arguments. Simple arguments usually start with a statement and end with a conclusion. Here is an example:

> If London is in England, then London is not in America.

> London is in England.

> Therefore, London is not in America.

The argument is said to be "valid" because if the first two statements are true, then the conclusion must be true. Here is another argument.

> All cats have fur.

> Bingo has fur.

> Therefore, Bingo is a cat.

This is an instance where the first two statements seem to be true, but the conclusion is not valid because it is not proven by the statements. Bingo could be a cat, but Bingo could also be a dog or any other animal with fur. Invalid arguments such as this are called fallacies.

ENTER THE MATRIX

There are many different kinds of logic. Computer science, mathematics, and other studies are forms of logic that use special types of language, symbols, and diagrams. Sometimes diagrams can be used to work out everyday problems as well. One diagram is called

Critical factors	Weight	Stay	Job A	Job B
Match my passion	200	7	9	8
Compensation & benefit	30	7	7	8
Quality time with family	25	8	9	6
Sustainability	15	7	6	9
Career progression	10	8	7	8
TOTAL SCORE	**100**	**735**	**775**	**765**

This decision matrix helped someone decide whether to remain at his current job or take a different position. After weighing the factors, he determined that Job A was the best option.

a decision matrix. Here is how a decision matrix might help with that problem of an overcrowded schedule.

Suppose the student is wondering which activity in his busy schedule might have to go in order to free up more time for study, plus allow for some free time on the weekends. He could list the activities in a line across the top of a blank page. The line would include work, sports, study, hanging out with friends, and gaming— all activities that take up allotments of time. On the left side of the page, there would be a column of all the valuable aspects of each of those activities. These might include money, prestige, fun, good grades, and making parents happy.

Next, each of those valuable or important aspects would be assigned a factor from one to three, with three equaling the most valuable thing. If the student really needs money, that item would get a three. If money is not a priority at the time, then that column would only receive a one. How important is getting good grades? A one, a two, or a three?

Then, in the space under each activity, a value from one to ten would be assigned, cross-referencing all the things that are important about it. If all the student's money comes from work, then work would get a ten. If the job is somewhat fun, that column might get a four or five. Since only professional athletes get paid for playing sports, a zero would go on the money line for that activity.

The next would be to multiply each value by its importance factor and add the results under each activity. What are the scores for each? High scores indicate the items that matter the most, while low scores show someone what activities might be eliminated from a busy schedule or at least the activities on which a person could spend less time. This is a case of using mathematical logic to solve the problem of the busy schedule.

HOW DOES IT FEEL?

Logic is a great problem-solving tool, but it cannot solve every problem. Did you ever hear somebody say, "I know it makes sense, but it just doesn't feel right"? Even the most logical people have emotions, and sometimes feelings just cannot be set aside when it is time to make a decision. In fact, some scientists who study the human brain have suggested that emotion is even more important than logic when it comes to making decisions because the brain is just wired that way.

It is one thing to make a logical decision, but that doesn't always mean that it is the best decision. When others are involved, it is important to consider their feelings, too, especially if their cooperation is needed to carry out the decision.

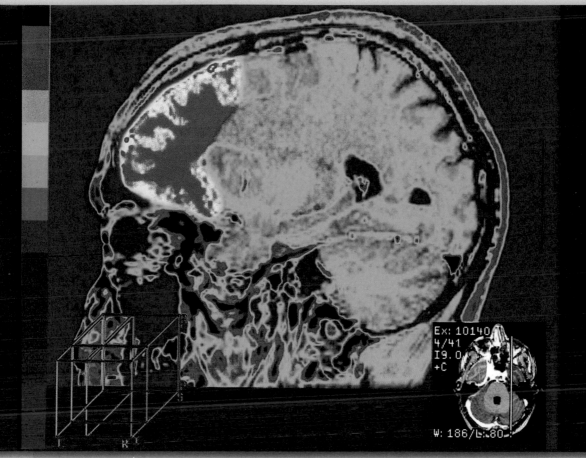

This magnetic resonance imaging (MRI) scan of the human brain indicates emotional activity in the frontal lobe, which is the part of the brain where decisions are made.

BEWARE OF BIAS

Biases are different from emotions. Bias is a tendency to think in certain ways, and it sometimes leads people to make decisions that in reality won't work. Psychologists have identified dozens of different kinds of biases.

Sometimes people are biased toward taking action when they feel pressure to do something about a situation. They may think of the positive outcomes and forget about some of the possible negative consequences. This kind of bias can be overcome by pausing to look at the risks and carefully considering alternative plans.

Sometimes people are biased because of peer pressure. They feel compelled to do what their friends or others around them do, and they tend to practice what is known as "groupthink," or a pattern of thought guided by conformity to group values. Another form of bias is simply reluctance to change or an unwillingness to try anything different. These kinds of biases make it hard to choose creative solutions or to think outside the box.

One way to counter those kinds of biases is to bounce ideas off a trusted person outside the group, or even multiple people, if possible. It can be even more helpful if that person doesn't know much about the situation and is hearing it explained for the first time. This can lead to fresh thoughts and new alternatives.

The desire to get what we want right now, also known as instant gratification, is a strong bias that influences almost everyone. It prompts people to do things such as spend their savings on frivolous purchases, rather than leaving savings untouched to have more money for something better or more meaningful in the future.

One way to overcome the instant gratification urge is to delay making a decision. This is a good option if a problem is not urgent. If possible, reward yourself for delaying by doing another activity you enjoy.

MAKING IT HAPPEN

The final step in the problem-solving process is putting a decision into practice. The previous steps were all about thinking, but this one is about doing. One of the best tools for putting decisions into practice is through forming an action plan.

The first step is to list each thing that needs to be done in order to make a decision work. Then the list should continue on to each

Instant gratification leads many people to choose spending over saving. But if you take the time to weigh your options, you may decide that saving money for later is worth it.

subsequent step. Each of these steps should be marked with the day on which it will be started, as well as the day on which it will be completed. If some things seem too big to accomplish all at once, they can be broken down into smaller steps and taken on one at a time.

Smart problem solving includes thinking about the problems and obstacles that are likely to be faced and how they can be overcome. It also includes considering what could be done if the obstacles prove to be too big or if something unexpected comes up. What is the worst that could happen?

It's impossible to predict the future. That is why it's always a good idea to make a contingency plan, or what is known as a "plan B." Think about each step in the first plan and the things that could possibly go wrong in the course of that plan. Then map out another step-by-step strategy for reaching the goal.

Once the steps in plan A are under way, it's also important to review each one and see how well it is working. Just as we learn from problems themselves, any mistakes that might come up are a good opportunity to think about how to avoid them in the future. It is also a good idea to look at any new ideas or opportunities that might have come up since the plan was put into action. Readiness to change the plan to deal with both the bad and the good things that might happen is key to victory.

Chapter 5

PROBLEMS WITH PROBLEM SOLVING

Problems can create opportunities to make things better, as Sir Alexander Fleming discovered when he returned to his messy lab. However, these opportunities can be missed by failing to use imagination, being closed-minded, or failing to keep an eye on how the solution is working.

There are several sure ways not to solve a problem. One is pretending that there is nothing wrong. Another common one is procrastinating, or putting off taking any action to solve it. Of course, sometimes things also just go wrong. Surprises can happen even if somebody has correctly defined the problem, come up with brilliant alternative solutions, made an informed decision, put together a great action plan, and worked hard to make it happen.

There are many problems, and countless ways to solve them. There are also plenty of ways that problem solving itself can go wrong. Just realizing that things can go haywire, however, can help people head off problematic problem solving.

It's easy to put off studying, but procrastination only makes it harder to motivate yourself to do the work later.

WHEN DOING NOTHING ISN'T AN OPTION

Problems can be scary things, and sometimes it seems that the best thing to do is to try to forget about them and hope they will go away. They can also be complicated, and there are times when it looks like finding a perfect solution is nearly impossible.

Looking at problems as scary or unsolvable, or hoping for the "perfect" solution, can lead to procrastination, which is putting off

THE QUICK FIX

People would have a hard time surviving without being able to react in emergencies. Sometimes major problems appear so suddenly and are so dangerous that a solution has to be found, and there is no time to plan or consider alternatives. Even when there is no emergency in sight, there may be a lot of pressure to solve a problem quickly. People face deadlines with work and school all the time.

In his book *The Slow Fix*, author Carl Honoré argues that it is best to go slow whenever possible in trying to solve complex problems. Being patient allows time to learn from mistakes, find root causes of problems, work with others, and try new things.

He says that quick fixes can also backfire. For example, people spend billions of dollars on diet products to lose weight, even though more and more people are becoming obese. That's because there is no such thing as a quick fix for obesity. Studies show that most people who lose weight on fad diets regain it, and often more than they lost to begin with, within five years. A healthier approach is a prolonged period of diet and exercise, even if it takes longer or proves to be more work.

While quick fixes are the right answer for some immediate problems, there are no shortcuts to solving major problems like obesity, global warming, broken relationships, or troubles in business, economics, and politics.

This figure skater listens to her music and visualizes her routine before performing it in front of an audience.

action until later. While it's true that sometimes problems go away on their own, mostly they do not. In fact, sometimes failing to act just makes things worse.

People put off taking action when they are afraid of failing, when they are afraid of doing something wrong, or when they simply lack self-control. The good news is that there are several ways to beat it.

One way to overcome procrastination is to break down a problem into the smallest parts possible and then implement a good action plan to tackle those components one by one. Whenever a person actually starts an activity, the mind keeps urging him or her to finish it. Then, once that activity is done, there is a sense of relief. Doing one item in the action plan each day, even if it takes just a few minutes, helps overcome procrastination and motivates somebody to push forward toward a solution.

Visualization is another trick that can keep a person moving toward the goal. Athletes often do visualization to help their performance, even during competition. A golfer takes a practice swing and imagines how he'll hit the ball. A kicker in football will follow through once or twice before actually attempting a field goal. These techniques motivate the athletes to perform well.

It's also helpful to visualize conversations or other things that have to be done in order to carry out a plan of action. It is important not only to imagine a successful outcome, but also to use imagination to see, hear, and feel the obstacles that will arise and how they can be overcome. Visualization works best when a person can imagine the details of what lies ahead—sights, the feel of things, the sounds, and even the smell of a scenario. People are more likely to take action when they have written down what they plan to do. That's another reason why a written action plan helps head off procrastination.

It is also important for a person to remember to reward himself or herself each time he or she completes a step of the plan.

Going to the movies with friends is one way to reward yourself for moving toward your goal.

It doesn't have to be a big reward. A movie, a good meal, or even a favorite snack can count as a mental payoff for work done and can keep a person moving.

PEOPLE AND PATIENCE

Many problems can't be solved without the help of others. But what if they refuse to help? People cannot always get what they want, but when dealing with others, it pays to be prepared. Including important people in the planning process can make them a part of the solution. And a great way to include them is simply to listen. Listening carefully to what people say makes them feel respected and builds trust. It is a way of letting them know that their concerns are important.

Before approaching someone for input, it may be a good idea to think of questions to ask. Rather than starting with a direct request, such as "Will you do this for me?" it may be better to ask, "Can you think of a way I might solve this problem?" or "What do you think of this idea?" Depending on the answers, it may be possible to work with that person toward the best possible out-come for both parties involved—a win-win solution.

Good salespeople know what their customers want and need. They spend a lot of time gathering as much information about them as possible so they can discuss things they may have in common and win their confidence. If they don't make a sale at first, skilled salespeople try to leave the door open for the future by asking questions like, "Can we discuss it again later?"

To get someone's help solving a problem or accepting a solution, sometimes it pays to act like a salesperson. If someone isn't willing to cooperate, that doesn't automatically mean that the problem is impossible to solve. It just means there is more information to be learned that may help find a new angle to the problem, either now or sometime in the future. Gathering

Even if a salesman does not manage to sell his product today, his positive interaction with the prospective client could lead to success next time.

information helps people weigh their alternatives.

Talking out problems with other people, learning from mistakes, making and revising plans, and subsequently carrying them out may seem like a long process. Some problems, of course, just cannot wait. If someone has a minor accident at home and is bleeding badly, a friend would do all he or she could to stop the bleeding, probably by applying a bandage. That is an example of a quick fix, and quick fixes are often necessary in emergencies. They may relieve the main problem, but they're not always a permanent solution, and they often relieve symptoms without dealing with the root problem. That person, for example, might need a follow-up visit to a doctor or hospital to check for infections or to better bandage the wound.

The *Apollo 13* crisis is another great example of many quick fixes that were put in place to bring the astronauts home safely. Nevertheless, the main problem wasn't solved until investigators combed through the crippled ship and found a fault in the wiring. They were then able to develop long-term solutions to prevent the problem from recurring on future missions.

Nothing stays permanently the same. Even the best plan can go wrong if it is ignored and left to work on its own. That is why it is essential from time to time to take a fresh look at solutions to problems. Sometimes a solution may have been fair to everyone at first, but after a period of time, new problems crop up. That means it's time for new solutions. Some diagrams for problem solving are drawn in circles, showing that the process never really stops. It just repeats again as time passes.

"Practice makes perfect" is an old saying that can be applied to problem solving. While the solutions themselves will rarely be enduringly perfect, repeated problem solving will help fine-tune your skills to become an excellent problem solver—one who can accurately identify problems, come up with possible solutions, effectively enact them, and follow up on their progress. While solutions themselves must change and adapt for new problems, the upside is that there will always be plenty of opportunities to practice. With all of that practice, anyone can become an expert at problem solving and succeed beyond expectations at school, at work, or in life!

GLOSSARY

alternative One of the possibilities for a choice that must be made.

bias Prejudice for or against something; an inclination.

brainstorming A problem-solving technique in which a group comes up with and shares multiple ideas.

compromise An agreement in which all sides agree to give up certain demands.

contingency An event in the future whose occurrence cannot be predicted with certainty.

counterintuitive Something different than what intuition would suggest or that is against natural logic or assumptions.

definition A statement of the exact meaning of something.

evaluate To determine the value of something.

gratification The sense of pleasure derived from getting what one wants; satisfaction.

groupthink Used to describe a decision influenced by conformity to a group rather than by individual will or beliefs.

intuition Sensing or understanding something without conscious reasoning.

involved Being connected with something or someone, or forming a part of it.

negotiation Discussion that seeks to give all parties something they seek in order to solve a problem.

obstacle Something that blocks progress or achievement.

perspective A point of view; a way of looking at something.

priority The importance of something in relation to other things.

procrastination Putting off or delaying a task until a later time.

reluctance Demonstration of doubt or the unwillingness to do something.

validity The quality of being logically correct or founded on truth.

visualization Using imagination to picture a scene or situation.

FOR MORE INFORMATION

Academic Games Leagues of America (AGLOA)
P.O. Box 17563
West Palm Beach, FL 33416
(561) 624-1884
Website: http://agloa.org
AGLOA is a nonprofit academic organization promoting
    advanced, problem-solving-based thinking in students
    throughout the United States. It hosts interschool competi-
    tions and a national championship tournament based on a
    series of language arts-, history-, and mathematics-based
    games designed to promote critical thinking.

Creative Problem Solving Society (CPSS)
P.O. Box 18101
RPO Heritage Mountain
Port Moody, BC V3H 0A2
Canada
Website: http://www.odysseybc.ca/index.php/contact
The CPSS is a nonprofit society based out of Canada that seeks
    to provide opportunities for creative and innovative
    thinkers to develop ideas and dialogue on problem-solving
    skills and abilities, in the context of education and
    day-to-day life.

Future Problem Solving Program International, Inc. (FPSPI)
2015 Grant Place
Melbourne, FL 32901
(800) 256-1499
Website: http://www.fpspi.org

The FPSPI is an organization dedicated to stimulating critical-
and creative-thinking skills in students worldwide, with
the goal of developing problem-solving skills applicable to
future global problems. The skills promoted by the program can be applied to school, the workplace, and broader
societal issues.

Odyssey of the Mind
c/o Creative Competitions, Inc.
406 Ganttown Road
Sewell, NJ 08080
(856) 256-2797
Website: http://www.odysseyofthemind.com
The Odyssey of the Mind program is an international organization that promotes critical-thinking skills in students via
problem-solving exercises. With programs in schools at all
grade levels, the organization also hosts competitions and
provides resources for team-building challenges and other
classroom-friendly exercises.

Services for Youth
Attn: Youth Operations Directorate
140 Promenade du Portage, Phase IV, 4D392
Mail Drop 403
Gatineau, QC K1A 0J9
Canada
(800) 935-5555
Website: http://www.youth.gc.ca
The government of Canada's Services for Youth helps young
people identify their career interests, find the training and
education necessary for their interests, and find employ-
ment opportunities. It also promotes skill development

and common problem-solving techniques useful for school and work.

SkillsUSA
14001 SkillsUSA Way
Leesburg, VA 20176
(703) 777-8810
Website: http://www.skillsusa.org
SkillsUSA is a partnership of students, teachers, and industry that helps young people prepare and develop the necessary skills to join the work force. It has programs and activities to foster creativity, problem solving, and other essential workplace skills

WEBSITES

Due to the changing nature of Internet links, Rosen Publishing has developed an online list of websites related to the subject of this book. This site is updated regularly. Please use the following link to access the list:

http://www.rosenlinks.com/WAWR/Solv

FOR FURTHER READING

Autry, James A. *The Book of Hard Choices: How to Make the Right Decisions at Work and Keep Your Self-Respect*. New York, NY: Morgan Road, 2006.

Breeze, Maureen, and Carol Carter. *Critical and Creative Thinking for Teenagers*. Denver, CO: LifeBound, 2010.

Burrow-Sanchez, Jason. *Adapt: Advancing Decision Making and Problem Solving for Teens*. Eugene, OR: Pacific Northwest Publishing, 2013.

Carter, Patricia, and David Carter. *Critical Thinking: A Guide for Teens*. Seattle, WA: Amazon Digital Services, 2013.

Fisher, Alex. *Critical Thinking: An Introduction*. New York, NY: Cambridge University Press, 2011.

Fox, Marci G., and Leslie Sokol. *Think Confident, Be Confident for Teens: A Cognitive Therapy Guide to Overcoming Self-Doubt and Creating Unshakable Self-Esteem*. Oakland, CA: New Harbinger Publications, 2011.

Givler, Ray. *Don't Get Fooled!: How to Analyze Claims for Fallacies, Biases, and Other Deceptions*. Seattle, WA: Amazon Digital Services, 2013.

Harmon, Daniel E. *Frequently Asked Questions About Overscheduling and Stress* (FAQ: Teen Life). New York, NY: Rosen Publishing Group, 2010.

Kahaner, Ellen. *Great Communication Skills* (Work Readiness). New York, NY: Rosen Publishing, 2008.

Kaplan, Arie. *Social Intelligence* (The 7 Character Strengths of Highly Successful Students). New York, NY: Rosen Publishing, 2013.

Konnikova, Maria. *Mastermind: How to Think Like Sherlock Holmes*. New York, NY: Viking, 2013.

La Bella, Laura. *Curiosity* (The 7 Character Strengths of Highly Successful Students). New York, NY: Rosen Publishing, 2013.

Robinson, Matthew. *Making Smart Choices About Time Management (*Making Smart Choices*)*. New York, NY: Rosen Publishing Group, 2008.

Sommer, Carl. *Teen Success in Career & Life Skills*. Houston, TX: Advance Publishing, 2009.

Sommers, Michael A. *Great Interpersonal Skills* (Work Readiness). New York, NY: Rosen Publishing, 2008.

Watanabe, Ken. *Problem Solving 101: A Simple Book for Smart People*. New York, NY: Penguin Group, 2009.

Wilson, Michael R. *Frequently Asked Questions About How the Teen Brain Works* (FAQ: Teen Life). New York, NY: Rosen Publishing, 2009.

Zegarelli, Mark. *Logic for Dummies*. Hoboken, NJ: Wiley Publishing, 2007.

BIBLIOGRAPHY

Baldwin, Stanley. *Take This Job & Love It*. Downers Grove, IL: InterVarsity Press, 1988.

Brezina, Corona. *Great Decision-Making Skills (*Work Readiness*)*. New York, NY: Rosen Publishing, 2008.

Hirsh, Sandra Krebs. *Work It Out: Clues for Solving People Problems at Work*. Palo Alto, CA: Davies-Black Publishing, 1996.

Honore, Carl. *The Slow Fix: Solve Problems, Work Smarter, and Live Better in a World Addicted to Speed*. New York, NY: HarperCollins Publishing, 2013.

Markkula Center for Applied Ethics. "Ethical Decision Making." Santa Clara University. Retrieved Jan. 15, 2014 (http://www .scu.edu/ethics/practicing/decision/homepage7.html? utm_expid=6222598-4.JgZsUfB3QmOXiTChyLdBfw .7&utm_referrer=http%3A%2F%2Fethicsops.com%2F EthicsTestsIDEthicsIssue.php).

Markman, Arthur B. *Smart Thinking: Three Essential Keys to Solve Problems, Innovate, and Get Things Done*. New York, NY: Perigree, 2012.

Nalebuff, Barry, and Ian Ayres. *Why Not? How to Use Everyday Ingenuity to Solve Problems Big and Small*. Boston, MA: Harvard Business School Publishing, 2003.

Quick, Thomas L. *Unconventional Wisdom: Irreverent Solutions to Tough Problems at Work*. San Francisco, CA: Jossey-Bass, 1989.

Reinhold, Ross. "Zig-Zag Problem Solving Model." PersonalityPathways. Retrieved Dec. 27, 2013 (http://www .personalitypathways.com/article/problemsolve.html).

Rykersmith, Eva. "Five Biases in Decision Making." The Fast Track, Intuit. June 7, 2013. Retrieved Jan. 4, 2014 (http:// quickbase.intuit.com/blog/2013/06/07/5-biases-in-decision -making-part-2).

Stone, Florence M. *The Essential New Manager's Kit*. Chicago, IL: Dearborn Trade Publishing, 2004.

Thompson Leigh. *The Truth About Negotiations*. Upper Saddle River, NJ: Pearson Education, 2013.

U.S. Department of Labor. "Problem Solving and Critical Thinking." Skills to Pay the Bills. Retrieved Nov. 13, 2013. (http://www.dol.gov/odep/topics/youth/softskills/Problem.pdf).

Vergano, Dan. "Study: Emotion Rules the Brain's Decisions." *USA Today*. Aug. 6, 2006. Retrieved Dec. 17, 2014 (http://usa today30.usatoday.com/tech/science/discoveries/2006 -08-06-brain-study_x.htm).

INDEX

A

alternatives
    devising as step in problem
      solving, 15
arguments
    structure of, 36
Apollo 13, 7–9, 11, 19–20, 50

B

bias, 39–40
brainstorming, 18, 26–29
Briggs, Katharine Cook, 18
bullying, 11
business consultants, 18

C

compromising, 30
contingency plans, 42

D

decision making
    as step in problem solving,
      15, 18
    putting the decision into
      practice, 40–42
decision matrix, 37–38
diagrams, 12, 36–38
doctors
    problem solving methods
      of, 20

E

Einstein, Albert, 16
emergencies, 45, 50
experience
    as factor in problem solv-
      ing, 6

F

feedback, 49
feeling
    as means of decision making,
      38–40
    as personality type, 18
Fleming, Alexander, 13, 43
Follett, Mary Parker, 32

G

goals, 29–30
groupthink, 40

H

Honoré, Carl, 45

I

identification
    as step in problem solving, 12
imagination
    as step in problem solving,
      19, 26
instant gratification, 40

ABOUT THE AUTHOR

Larry Gerber, a former Associated Press bureau chief, has worked in employee recruitment and training for several organizations in the United States and abroad. He has written important books on career preparedness and critical thinking for Rosen, including *Top 10 Tips for Developing Money Management Skills* and *The Distortion of Facts in the Digital Age*. He lives in Los Angeles.

PHOTO CREDITS